SIST.

INS   NS

First published in 2012 by

the columba press

55A Spruce Avenue, Stillorgan Industrial Park,
Blackrock, Co. Dublin
www.columba.ie

ISBN 978-185-607-800-9

Design by Emer O Boyle

Printed by MPG Books Group Limited

Sr Stanislaus Kennedy

Sr Stan's book of
INSPIRATIONS

The Sanctuary, a meditation centre in the heart of Dublin city, was founded in 1998 by Sr Stanislaus Kennedy. It has been evolving around its vision – to be ... STILLNESS ... in the world. The Sanctuary believes that everyone – the child, the teenager, the adult – can access this place of stillness within themselves and that once it is part of their consciousness, its potential for their well-being and the well-being of society is huge.

www.sanctuary.ie

INTRODUCTION

This little book is meant for everyone who wishes to read it. It isn't written to convince you about anything. It is a book to have by your side, in your bag, in your pocket or at your bedside. Pick it up and put it down as you please.

It is not a book to be read sequentially. It is not about bringing you new ideas that you might play around with, analyse or criticise. Read the reflections and aphorisms in your own way and in your own time. Allow them to speak to your heart; to create a silence within you; to reveal their message to you; to draw you ever more deeply into the journey of life. It is simply intended that this little book will bring you into a deeper part of your being, the still point where Thomas Merton has said:

"God has written his name on us."

JANUARY

JANUARY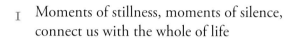

1 Moments of stillness, moments of silence, connect us with the whole of life

2 Each dawn a genesis, a new beginning, a resurrection, a promise

3 Snow – a painted landscape calling me to stillness

4 Creation speaks to our hearts when we listen

Standing on the shore, part of the rhythm
of the tide. Each wave a giving and a
taking, impermanence dissolving into
permanence

5

The journey of the river is like the
journey of the soul, feeding itself from its
own source

6

The bounty of the universe begins with
the gift of life

7

Nature: we are part of it, living it,
breathing it. It is part of us,
encompassing us, holding us in its heart

8

JANUARY

9
A flower opening to morning light,
closing as the light fades: a daily miracle

※

10
The material world is our way to
contact divine life; every tiny little bit of
it a glimpse into the soul of eternity

※

11
Surrendering completely to sound we
discover sacred stillness

※

12
Life is a series of experiences through
which we can come to know our true
selves

JANUARY

When we acknowledge another with
full and unconditional attention
we meet ourselves

13

Maturity combines the fresh
enthusiasm of youth with the wisdom
of age

14

Joy comes in little whispers, in sudden
unexpected glimpses

15

Memories are our greatest treasure,
always present in any space,
in every place

16

JANUARY

17 The more we discover the more we have
    to learn

---

18 Our search is ongoing, our journey
    unfinished

---

19 Every step on our journey is a return to
    the beginning

---

20 In learning not to fear uncertainty we
    discover inner strength

JANUARY

When I know that enough is enough
I will have enough always

⊱∞∞⊰

Our unlived lives, our undreamt
dreams, our greatest loss is the life we
allow to die while we live

⊱∞∞⊰

Life is simple and serene when it is
lived from the heart with integrity

⊱∞∞⊰

The beginning and end of our journey
is finding our true selves

JANUARY

25   Living life is not automatic: we must choose to live it

---

26   Living with integrity, we bring body, mind and spirit into everything

---

27   Courage is a gift of the heart. It opens us to experience, stirs us to compassion, and frees our creativity

---

28   Life is about giving and receiving, moment by moment

JANUARY

Our humanity calls us in our poverty
to make the world a better place

29

A life of love is a choice we make

30

We all long to feel real, yet we fear it.
We run away even as we are irresistibly
drawn to it

31

FEBRUARY

FEBRUARY

I   Neighbourliness: a sacred gift in a torn world

---

2   There is another way to live in this noisy, distracted world and it is not as out of reach as it may seem

---

3   There is no limit to wakefulness: no one wakes up once and for all

---

4   To live from the heart is to love fully

FEBRUARY

The purpose of this day is to discover
who we are and what we are called to be

5

The purpose of this day is to find the joy
we are born to know

6

It is only in losing ourselves that we find
our true selves

7

The wonder moments of life keep our
hearts alive and sustain us in dark times

8

FEBRUARY

9   All life is connected at the core, flowing from the same source – the divine river of life

---

10   In the here, in the now – an eternal moment

---

11   Living in the moment we do not miss the present

---

12   Our destiny is here, it is now

FEBRUARY

FEBRUARY

17   Eternity is the overcoming of time by
the now that does not pass away

⸙

18   When we live in the moment we live in
and out of time

⸙

19   We are reborn each day, into a new time
with a new opportunity to respond to
yesterday's difficulties

⸙

20   When we listen to the silence of the
moment we hear the deep desires and
longings of our heart

FEBRUARY

FEBRUARY

25   Believing what is not seen, seeing what
is not visible, knowing the limits of our
life, we give thanks

⸙

26   Giving and receiving are one in
gratitude: we cannot give thanks for
what we have not taken to heart

⸙

27   Gratitude always gives more

⸙

28   At the core of our being is emptiness
and fullness, nothingness and
everything; there dwells the divine

FEBRUARY

When we allow surprise to flow in our   29
lives, we take nothing for granted

MARCH

MARCH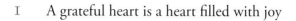

1   A grateful heart is a heart filled with joy

2   The child in us never dies

3   Gratefulness is being surprised by the ordinary

4   Every moment is given, every moment a gift

MARCH

Dignity is never diminished by
indifference or ill will

5

Absorbed in lighting a candle, watching
the flame flickering, we enter into the
stillness of the small circle of light

6

Beauty is found in solitude, in nature
and in the unfolding of the human heart

7

Only in stillness do we hear truth. Only
through stillness do we understand
truth. Only out of stillness do we speak
truth

8

MARCH

9   The soul is that place in us where love
and light, joy and peace, truth and
beauty abide

---

10   Awake, aware, beyond thought, pure
presence – stillness

---

11   We are infinitely more than we imagine,
infinitely greater than our mind

---

12   The spiritual life is a life of love, a life of
giving and receiving. It is never a solo
act

Living by measurements, achievements, ambitions, goals and expectations, we forget when enough is enough

13

It takes courage to follow the deepest desires of our heart, to say no to other people's plans for us, to leave other voices behind and to say yes to the quiet, still voice calling from within

14

Whenever anyone responds with love or kindness, wherever anyone seeks truth, peace or justice, there God is

15

God is always at work in us, even this very moment. What fluctuates is our openness and receptivity

16

MARCH

17 To be full, we must be empty

---

18 Letting go of the compulsion to be
    successful, to be right, to be in control,
    to be powerful, is the only way to
    freedom

---

19 We can only take with us when we die
    what we let go when we are alive

---

20 In letting go of life, we discover new life

MARCH

Ours is the choice – to live in trust or live in fear

⸻

We can overcome our fear only by letting go of it

⸻

Absorbed in ourselves, unaware of what life is offering, we are unable to receive the joys of the moment, the gifts of today

⸻

Entering into the night, we return into the silence that is the dark soil in which we are rooted

MARCH

25 The less we have, the easier it is to appreciate

---

26 If we learn to let go during life we will be able to die easily

---

27 Any time is a time to stop, live in the moment and accept what is

---

28 Indecision, holding back, standing on the edge of fear, breeds insecurity

When we live a detached life,
pretending to be something we are not,
we cannot live at ease with ourselves

29

When we accept our weakness
everything changes. The mirage of
control disappears and our weakness
becomes our strength

30

Night completes the circle of the hours
as death completes the circle of life

31

APRIL

APRIL

1   To let go, to be able to stand and leave
    everything behind without looking back,
    is to say yes to inner freedom

2   At birth, we are given an angel, a gift of
    courage. All we need to know is that it is
    there

3   Life is a river and if we learn to let go, not
    to cling to the banks, just to go with the
    flow, it carries us; it bears us up in trust

4   Death is the way into the divine presence,
    the resolution of a lifetime of wonder and
    waiting

APRIL

APRIL

9   This is one of the basic laws of life – that when we give we receive

---

10   As we connect, reconnect and interconnect, our lives are woven into unity

---

11   Tomorrow is the enemy of today, for we cannot be tomorrow what we can be today

---

12   Without love, justice is realism, hope is self-centredness, forgiveness is self-abasement, generosity is extravagance

APRIL

When we journey with awareness, each
event is unique, each step is the first step   13

When we hear the stillness in the heart
of the world, all creation becomes our   14
companion

In stillness I notice people around me,
who they are, who I am, where we are   15
going, how we journey together

Music arises out of silence into which   16
it inevitably flows

17 Joy is the experience of losing ourselves, of being emptied of self

18 Prayer is attuning ourselves to the flow of life

19 Sitting still, trying not to try, wanting not to want, not setting our heart on anything, we discover inner peace

20 Prayer changes us and in changing us it changes the world

When I stop, I find you. When I look, I
see you. When I listen, I hear you

21

Prayer is not working or straining the
mind; it is a simple matter of opening
the heart

22

This is how we learn to be still: by sitting
quietly, facing fear with trust, listening to
our own depth, allowing the dawn to rise
out of the night

23

Peace is found not only in the desert or
in some remote and silent monastery
but in the tumult of the marketplace and
the pulse of the human heart

24

25   Prayer is never a private matter. It is
always inclusive. It is opening our
hearts to the universe

26   Stillness accepts noise; then moves
beneath it to an inner silence

27   You are always in and around me,
always sheltering me, but it is only in
awareness that I experience you

28   We are one, you and I, bound together
in a covenant of peace, ringed around
in a circle of love

Silently listening to our breathing, we
are intimately at one with the life breath
of the universe

29

When we are too busy to be still our
ears and eyes are open only to projects
and plans, missing the wonder of the
moment

30

MAY

MAY

1   Forgiveness is a taste of divine grace – a
pure gift

2   Preserving the silence within amid all
the noise and clatter of life, we grow into
our true selves

3   Prayer is an opening of the heart that
takes us beyond our limited rational
mind, beyond the ego, the separate self,
into the transcendent mystery

4   Each morning blesses us with time and
space to be attentive to all that is new this
day

When the challenges of the day overwhelm us they can also remind us to stop, to catch our breath, to make sense, to take rest, to find strength in the moment

5

Before we sleep, gathering up all the day's contradictions, knitting together what is broken – a healing experience

6

Life is about moments

7

Receptivity: a condition of the night, a reminder of the often unrecognised virtue of lives lived in dependency, of lives lived in the service of others

8

MAY

9   Setting aside our day we enter serenity

---

10   Opening to our inner self frees us to
trust each new moment in time

---

11   Before turning on the computer,
opening the door, getting into the car,
answering the phone, let us stop, pause
and breathe, mindfully

---

12   Mortality reminds us to do what we do
well; happily, joyfully, freely living in the
now

MAY

Each dawn a gift, moving out of darkness into light

13

<hr />

Aspiring to be good, we inspire others to goodness

14

<hr />

There is never a moment that isn't an opportunity to make space for the new by letting go of the old

15

<hr />

Realising our potential, our gifts shine out as blessings

16

MAY

17 Pondering in our hearts creation's story, surrendering to the rhythms of the day and the night, we savour the now

---

18 Silence embraced, truth and beauty become visible

---

19 The wise composer allows music to crescendo, reach a climax and then – pause, rest, silence, nothing. In the silence, we hear the music

---

20 No one lives by chance. Everyone, everything has a purpose, a part to play in the grand design that is creation

MAY

Being alive is sufficient proof that we
are essential to all creation, to all time

21

A day lived in unity with nature is a day
flowing in the eternal interconnectedness
of creation

22

Our purpose this day is not finding
security and certainty, it is discovering
the very best that is within us

23

Learning to trust ourselves, following
our deepest desires, exploring the
recesses of our heart we become whole

24

MAY

25   The purpose of this day is to discover and accept who we are and what we are called to be

26   Our spiritual journey – the greatest human adventure

27   The silence of the night invites us to detach ourselves from the possession of the day, entrusting it and ourselves to the freedom of God

28   In detachment from things we are free from small-mindedness

MAY

In practising awareness we learn to take possession of ourselves

29

In letting go we learn to live with ambiguity

30

In living with questions we learn to wait for answers

31

JUNE

JUNE

1   Patient waiting in silence teaches us to believe in ourselves and transform problems into possibilities

---

2   Night-time: examining the day, being grateful, forgiving, confronting our fears. Looking back, we lean forward

---

3   Learning to accept and live with polarities, tensions, paradoxes and contradictions is the secret to wholeness

---

4   Accepting without understanding, honouring differences, finding unity in diversity we move into truth

JUNE

Being mindful, giving thanks for what is given we bring to mind what otherwise might go unnoticed

5

Giving thanks, we become less concerned with what is missing and more focused on sharing what we have

6

As a musician, athlete, dancer benefits from the discipline of routine, so we too – through a daily spiritual routine – will unfold and blossom with vitality, joy and sensitivity

7

The way of truth tests our heart, examines our motivation, challenges our commitment, and always bears fruit

8

JUNE

9   With gratitude we make peace with our world and everything in our life

---

10   Time in the evening connecting with ourselves and the splendour of the universe, we are transformed

---

11   When we are challenged to stay on the road, not to turn back, to trust our inner wisdom, we touch that sacred space within

---

12   Joy cannot be organised, cannot be planned. We need only desire it, seek it and it finds us

JUNE

Aware or unaware, we create our own solutions, our own reality by choice or by chance

13

<hr>

Joy is ours when we do what we really want to do in freedom and integrity of heart

14

<hr>

At the core of our being we are all one, as we touch and are touched by each other

15

<hr>

A life taken for granted never knows joy 16

JUNE

17 Accepting the mystery of our being –
not proving it but being it – we become
the self we were born to be

—

18 Creation: ongoing story, new
beginnings, nothing complete

—

19 Creation: always becoming, always
being shaped, never complete

—

20 Truth comes in pairs of opposites

JUNE

We are strong when we embrace our
weaknesses, we are teachers when we
can be taught

21

We enjoy others when we enjoy
ourselves, when we enjoy ourselves
we are wise

22

When we accept our own foolishness
we find true happiness

23

Many of us become what others tell us
we are

24

JUNE

25　Listening to the small voice within we discover the person we are called to be, in our delightful uniqueness

---

26　Living in the moment, we experience life

27　In stillness a flower blooms, in stillness it fades away

28　Moving out of darkness into light, a moment neither dark nor light, a time to delight

JUNE

Morning: birth of colour, leaf and flower newly risen, out of the night, out of the earth, leaving the darkness without regret

29

Growth happens in the fertile darkness where the rain falls and the seed opens no matter how many trample overhead

30

JULY

JULY

I The last darkness of night dissipates, the sun bursts over the horizon – every day a new miracle – rarely experienced, yet always there

2 Darkness before dawn, pregnant with light

3 The treasures of the earth are free and full of surprises

4 The earth speaks in magic – rainbows and waterfalls speak to the heart

In accepting the inevitability of death we
discover a new way of living

5

⸎

Life fuelling the universe, always
flowing into us, blessing us; flowing
through us, blessing others

6

⸎

It is in responding with a full heart that
we experience joy

7

⸎

Divine joy is in us, given to us out of
love, being born in us anew each day

8

JULY

9   Work dignifies our every day, enabling what is unlived in us to flower

---

10   The world is ever being created, each of us in the making as each moment we are transformed in love

---

11   Unlike other creatures, we struggle to become who we are, as we experience ourselves unfinished

---

12   When we face challenges we find meaning

The harvest of our lives is already within   13

With every gift comes opportunities.
Enjoying them to the full, we rejoice in   14
the gift of being alive

Time does not run out. It rises as water
in a well, to fullness   15

Only here in this moment is the mystery
of now   16

JULY

17 Bells: a timeless call to enter the now, to stop, to listen, to hear the message of this moment and give thanks

---

18 Dying daily, we move naturally into eternal life

---

19 Living in the now is an invitation to awaken our souls, to stop, to listen, to choose a different way

---

20 When we turn the point between time and now into creative tension, we live life to the fullest

We think we have no time, that we are
running out of time, that time is out
of our control. But time is eternal, and
we have all the time we need, always,
because all time is ours, now

21

Thank you for the ordinary gifts of every
day, evoking in me wonder and surprise

22

Praise is our response to glory. The more
open we are, the more glory shines out

23

Just for ten seconds in silence
remember those who loved the good
that grows within us, those who
wanted what was best for us, those who
encouraged us to become who we are

24

JULY

25 It is not enough to feel grateful – we must think gratefully, imagine gratefully, act gratefully

26 In giving we are replenished

27 Teach me to wait silently, untroubled and without fear but full of gratitude

28 We are blessed when we are open to the gifts of the day

JULY

Gratitude is an attitude making us alive
to what we have

29

Surprise cannot be planned or
controlled but it is always there when we
are open to it

30

Just as we see the sun in its rays, the
fountain in its waters, so we can see
the streams of divine power in the daily
graces flowing into our lives

31

AUGUST

AUGUST

1   A soul touched by the Spirit is like a tree touched by the sun

---

2   Creation, beginning of time, before time, in time, all time

---

3   Soul is the unifying force at the centre of our being, never changing in a constantly changing world

---

4   The divine is the depth dimension in human experience

AUGUST

Journeying in faith we are who we are in
God – no more, no less   5

⊶⧫⊷

A flame burning, snowflake falling, bud
opening, wheel spinning – the dynamic   6
of stillness

⊶⧫⊷

Divine grace is like a lantern on a dark
path – shining only to illuminate the next   7
step

⊶⧫⊷

Connecting with the spirit we open
ourselves to the force that drives the   8
universe

AUGUST

9   Spirituality integrates and transforms
    the material world

---

10 We need to learn to let go of ourselves
    and in letting go we find God in our
    heart's core

---

11 Reflecting on the brokenness and
    fragility of our day, we greet the silence
    of the night

---

12 Each moment, I am one with the force
    of life

AUGUST

AUGUST

17 The moment we die to ourselves is the moment we are fully alive

18 The word that we are is always in the process of being spoken, completed only in death

19 When we rise wholeheartedly to the challenges of the day we will be let go when it is time to leave it all behind

20 Blessed, we bless in our turn, in our way, on our way.

AUGUST

By faith we die forward into the
fullness of life and that is resurrection

21

Knowing light shines in the dark, we
come to know darkness itself as light

22

God is in the mountain. The mountain
is in God. I am in the mountain, and
the mountain is in me

23

The soul of the world is the pulse of the
unfathomable, the heartbeat of all
creation, mysterious, sacred beyond
words

24

AUGUST

25 Through you I rise – and you through me – into this new day we are making together

26 Evening, when we have forgotten how to pray, it is enough to give ourselves over, in trust, to the night

27 In night prayer we connect the end of the day with the end of life

28 True living means alive to God, alive to ourselves and alive to others

When we see with the heart, we discover
that there is no part of life that doesn't
contain a surprise

29

We live in a changing world – if we don't
change we die

30

Moments of stillness and peace are
always available. They are offered to
everyone. It is only a matter of being
aware

31

SEPTEMBER

SEPTEMBER

1 Remember, until you love yourself in small ways, you cannot change yourself in bigger ways

⟨⟨⟨⟩⟩⟩

2 Accepting our limitations, we experience a new freedom and a new serenity

⟨⟨⟨⟩⟩⟩

3 The difficulties, tensions, pressures of the commuter's morning dissipate at a glimpse of the morning sky

⟨⟨⟨⟩⟩⟩

4 Instead of wanting more, give thanks for the blessings you already have

SEPTEMBER

Through our compassion, we too can
change the world

5

———

Our inner beauty flows through our
eyes, our smiles, our expressions, our
gestures, our perceptions, our joy, our
care and our compassion

6

———

Take the time to stop, look, observe.
Beauty surrounds you

7

———

Nourish your body with healthy food
and exercise. Nourish your mind with
good literature, art and company.
Nourish your spirit with silence,
stillness and prayer

8

SEPTEMBER

9 Do not be concerned about things you cannot change. Concern yourself, rather, with what you can

---

10 If you recognise and do well what is needed today, the future will find you doing what is needed at that time

---

11 The present moment is all you are sure of. Living in the moment is living fully

---

12 Always wanting to be right closes the mind and heart. With an open mind and an open heart, we may not always be right, but we won't be wrong

SEPTEMBER

Moments when we bless and feel blessed
are moments when we are most alone,
yet most alive to everyone and everything   13

If we try not to look ahead to tomorrow,
but instead live today well, tomorrow will   14
be happier

Seeing with the mind, we see
possibilities and potential. Seeing with
the heart, we have insights into life's   15
deepest meanings

Rid yourself of anxiety and anger. Learn
to walk with joy. Enjoy yourself and your   16
own company

SEPTEMBER

17
Hope is promise. Hope is possibility.
Hope is about what is not yet. Hope is
about what you do not see, but you trust
is there

⬥

18
Carrying bags of anger and resentment
takes a lot of energy. Forgive, and you
will immediately feel lighter

⬥

19
Each moment is the place you arrive at
from your most recent past and from
which you step into the future

⬥

20
If we surrender to difficult situations,
we develop new ways of living. We learn
to hold what happens. We learn to deal
with it. We learn to learn from it

SEPTEMBER

Busyness can keep you from receiving
the joy of the moment, the joy of the day. 21

✦

Life is a gift that comes wrapped in what
you experience 22

✦

A rainbow, a pure gift, comes quite
unexpectedly, apparently from nowhere 23
– an invitation to stop and stare

✦

An easy ride can't teach you how to
handle a dangerous, bumpy road 24

SEPTEMBER

25 Forgive yourself, forgive others, and you will live your life as a free human being

26 Through listening, you can learn how to rise above adversity, and learn to truly value other people who are very different from you

27 Patience is the skill of understanding and respecting our own rhythms and those of others

28 No matter how painful life may be, we have internal resources to heal and grow into happiness

SEPTEMBER

Peace comes from the heart that knows
that all life is sacred and all human   29
beings are equal

Whats we see or presume to see, day after
day, constitutes who we are and colours   30
our whole life

OCTOBER

OCTOBER

1   When you really live in hope, you do not deny darkness or negativity or pain, but neither do you give in or resign yourself to it

2   It is impossible to know who you are unless you know where you belong

3   Happiness comes from loving yourself as you are

4   If your view is tired and stale, if everything you see appears empty, maybe it is because you yourself are empty

OCTOBER

OCTOBER

9   Resentment is a barrier to our growth. Forgiveness is the beginning of our freedom

———⌘———

10   Living in the now challenges our tendency to wait or delay until success is assured before beginning

———⌘———

11   Knowing a person's story softens our judgement, makes us more tolerant, and leads to peace

———⌘———

12   Night prayer: drawing us into the mystery of night. We gather our day, offering it back to God in gratitude

OCTOBER

OCTOBER

17 Everything has its time, and that is always now

⊶⊷

18 When we become more individualistic, we become more isolated

⊶⊷

19 Self-esteem, once truly acquired can never be lost

⊶⊷

20 The acknowledgement of impermanence is the key to life itself

OCTOBER

Life unfolds everywhere at its own pace 21

21

Prophets are people with their feet on the ground, but with their minds and hearts filled with fiery dreams 22

It is by facing our wounds that we discover what it is that gives our lives meaning 23

Old age, the harvest time of life, a time to gather experiences, to celebrate them, and to share them 24

OCTOBER

25 Being honest about our struggles, our fears and our hopes is the best gift we can pass on to others

---

26 Deep within each of us there is a knowing place. When we spend time there, we tend to the gifts that we have been given, we discover how fruitful our life has been and how much we can share with the world

---

27 The reaper in us lives and works out of love with no assurance of success

---

28 Now is the time for us to reach out and see beauty in life's becoming

OCTOBER

Some visions unfold in our sleep, some
in visionary, waking moments. Seizing
these moments, we dream new dreams

29

When our heart breaks out of its
protective shell we feel naked. It is in
this nakedness we taste the essential
nature of our existence

30

The earth's whispers are everywhere,
but only those who have slept and
dreamt with it can respond to its call

31

NOVEMBER

NOVEMBER

I   Solitude is not running away. Rather,
     solitude helps us to create communion,
     by taking others into our hearts, into our
     solitude

2   The more deeply we listen, the more we
     tune ourselves into the cry of our heart

3   It is only if we choose to be attentive
     that we open our hearts to the wonder of
     things

4   It is a strange paradox that the more we
     forget ourselves, the more we find
     ourselves

NOVEMBER

The virtue of attentiveness allows us to
enjoy the journey and the destination   5

When we let go of our time, all time is
ours because we are in the present   6
moment, in the now that transcends time

All we need is to be, to be present, to
believe, to love, to trust, because God is   7
breathing on us and through us

Moving from a place of stillness,
we are capable of having a right
understanding, making right judgements   8
and taking right actions

NOVEMBER

9 Hope doesn't need words or proofs or conditions. Hope accepts mystery and offers the gift of solid trust in the unknown

10 Simplicity clears our vision and allows us to see what we really need and what is really enough

11 Negativity is a great clutterer. It keeps us from receiving the joys of the moment, the joys of the day

12 While it is essential that we become more loving persons, it is equally important that we accept ourselves as we really are

NOVEMBER

We live a simple life when we do not
pretend to be something we are not.

———

To unclutter our lives is to open our
hearts, to create emptiness where
fullness becomes possible

———

Today we can give away something we
treasure which would enrich the life of
somebody else and liberate ours

———

The greatest gift we can bring to another
is to open up to them their hidden
reservoir of love

NOVEMBER

17 Evening: a time to reflect on what we need, what we can let go, and what we can gather together before moving on

---

18 The heart stands for the centre of our being, where we are at one with ourselves, one with others, and one with that pure spirit of love that some of us call God

---

19 The loss of a loved one is a gap in the heart forever, because a door in our life closes that can never be opened by anyone else

---

20 No matter how close we get to one another, you can never know what it is like to be me and I can never know what it is like to be you

NOVEMBER

The journey of self-knowledge and self-acceptance is finding and accepting the great mystery that we are

This is the struggle of a lifetime, accepting the me within whom lies great beauty and great possibilities

It is precisely at the point of acceptance of our fragility and our brokenness that true development and growth can take place

The greater our awareness of each moment, the more we can let go of the stories that control our life

NOVEMBER

25 The less we assume, the more we are surprised and delighted with what we discover in the world

———— ✺ ————

26 The surprise of the unexpected will wear off, but the surprise of freshness never wears off

———— ✺ ————

27 When compassion becomes the foundation of our attitude to others, we see them with a fresh gaze and an open heart

———— ✺ ————

28 There is plenty for all of us – for you and for me – if only we have the eyes to see and the ears to hear and the heart to feel the gifts within us and around us

NOVEMBER

The way to heal a greedy, envious or demanding heart is to replace it with a grateful heart

29

When we are grateful, our lives will begin to change instantly and we will see clearly

30

DECEMBER

DECEMBER

I   In giving gifts, we often give what we can spare, but in giving thanks, we give ourselves

---

2   Even if our life lacks the surprise of the extraordinary, the ordinary can always be surprising

---

3   One spurt of surprise can lead to a blaze of gratefulness

---

4   Our forgiveness may not always be accepted, but once we have reached out our hand we rid ourselves of resentment

DECEMBER

If we cannot live at peace amidst the problems of our daily surroundings, we're not likely to make peace with the significant wounds and traumas of our life

5

───⟨≈≈⟩───

If we are successful in the denial of our pain, we create the illusion that it is under control. But that is not healing; it is merely temporary containment

6

───⟨≈≈⟩───

We can only bring compassion to others if we have experienced it ourselves

7

───⟨≈≈⟩───

Tenderness does not mean sentimentality; rather, it is unearthing gentleness and kindness, which shows that we consider other people to be important and precious

8

DECEMBER

9   It is important to hold memories of
goodness, to draw from them the
goodness in us; to catch it, to dwell on it,
to savour it

※

10   Being people of light and hope means
being willing to stay open to our fears

※

11   Many of us are just flickering wicks that
need to be pared and cared for, very
gently, carefully and confidently

※

12   Peace comes when we have met and
accepted the best and the worst within
us

DECEMBER

When we know what goes on in our
own heart we become more accepting,
tolerant and more open

13

We can only become peace-filled people
if we first acknowledge our own
propensity to violence and learn from it

14

If we are in harmony with ourselves, we
are in harmony with the movement of
the whole universe

15

When we smile, life is good and
goodness is all around us and that
makes us more gentle with ourselves
and with others

16

DECEMBER

17 Whether we are conscious of it or not, we all carry responsibility for the good and evil in our world today

---

18 Learning more about the great poverty and brokenness of our lives, we are also learning more about our potential and strength and the source of it

---

19 When we are too caught up with our projects and programmes, we miss out on the important things, our inner resources

---

20 Hope is living our dreams even when we experience failure and self-doubt

DECEMBER

Loss in nature is also loss for humanity,
and we are all responsible for
maintaining the harmony of the universe

21

The pain of life accepted with courage
awakens our love, stirs our compassion,
opens our mind – a gift of the heart

22

There is nothing – no person, no thing,
no thought, no experience, no sadness
or joy – nothing too small or nothing too
great that cannot be gathered and used
for the nourishment and beauty and
good of all

23

As we walk life's journey, realising that
we are connected with all that has gone
before and all that is present, we are
preparing for what is to come

24

DECEMBER

25   Wisdom is not knowing as well as knowing, and being at peace with that uncertainty

———✺———

26   Some of us have a blind hardness that quickly surfaces when our patch is threatened. It is prayer that softens our hardened hearts

———✺———

27   When we dare to see with the eyes of the soul, we begin to see sharper images, and our intuitive powers grow

———✺———

28   Life is an art. The art lies not in what we experience in life – but in how we harmonise our experiences

Just before sunrise the world takes a
deep breath, a crescendo of twitters
salute the day

29

Dawn chorus, exhaling new life echoing
over the earth

30

Pause, reflect, catch your breath, make
peace, find joy – in the moment

31